My Painting Speaks

OrangeBooks Publication

Smriti Nagar, Bhilai, Chhattisgarh - 490020

Website: **www.orangebooks.in**

© Copyright, 2022, Author

All rights reserved. No part of this book may be reproduced, stored in a retrieval system, or transmitted, in any form by any means, electronic, mechanical, magnetic, optical, chemical, manual, photocopying, recording or otherwise, without the prior written consent of its writer.

First Edition, 2022
ISBN: 978-93-5621-070-7

MY PAINTING SPEAKS

SMITA RAVISHANKAR

OrangeBooks Publication
www.orangebooks.in

Acknowledgement

I wish to thank everyone who involve somehow in my story during my journey, and I thanks to my Mom.

I thank God for providing the inspiration and Resources to accomplish this goal. God had been a great friend and helper throughout my journey, and the most supportive Mom.

The Universe has given guidance, and has given way to Pursue Inner Talent, Thank You God.

This could never be possible without "Orange Book Publication". Thank you, guys, for allowing me to publish this book from your Publications. Thanks to web site pixabay.com for free image library for digital print I collect few images from pixabay.com.

And Thanks To Readers for Choosing and Reading This Book.

Smita Ravishankar

Prologue

It Is a Unique Story, The Art warns us of dangerous trends, every picture playing the character inside the painting also has a tragic ending.

The Little Bird went, digging the mountain to save someone's child. saw someone burning in the coals, saw someone laughing far away.

by drawing the experiences, in the form of painting. and feeling it with experience, that feeling has been presented, like every art saying something, Leaf inside the book its future is, means tomorrow is, it is dried.

The Tears of a Tree, The Effort of a Bird, walking in sleeping position. a shadow, replica on the roof of water, there were no colours and changing colours. colours exist but no life but After Someone's End Had to Paint.

I Reached Inside Every Picture, I Used to feel pain, sometimes scared, sometimes my colours change, because those experiences needed the changed.

Feeling Every Picture while painting, has given life to it, so that every picture says something.

About Book

This Is a wonderful unique book; The author has made her art a painting a vision of a life. The hypocrisy of the world celebrates happiness by destroying one's life regardless of one's life. From her own experience, she feels that pain in her painting. And in Some photography, I have given life in painting at this book.

About Book

*S*he Emerges from The Caves, Stops on The Face, Sometimes She Yearns for A Drop of Water, Sometimes Gets Immersed in Water, Sometimes the Colours for Painting Are Finished, Sometimes Music Coming Out of The Water, Making A Shape with The Smoke,

She Saw the Living Tree Being Cut Down; She Saw the Dead Riding. She Got Drenched in Change, Saw the Somethings Moving, Walking in Sleeping Position,

Saw Someone Smiling Wrapped in The Embers of Fire, When Seen a Small Bird Digging a Mountain to Save Someone's Life. Every Picture in This Book Tells Something. "My Painting Speaks.

About Author

*S*mita Ravishankar lives in Mumbai, the first book is 'A Fascinating Journey with Spirit's", in which she has made her experience with spirits,

This book is very interesting as well as funny, scary, interesting, you will fall in love with the spirit of this book.

She got a lot of love from this book; this book was appreciated. It reached the heart of the reader, whoever got the book, they closed the book only after completing it.

While writing every sentence, she is written as much as she is writing for the first time. And she writes books and also writes for films. She amassed enough money to publish book.

In this book **"My Painting Speaks"** she stands in there, her life moving with every painting with every character.

About Author

*S*he is influenced by beauty wonders of nature, this question always remains in her mind that how this shape of smoke is formed, how fire got its shape, … that is living that moment and we can only see that moment from afar.

she had made every picture by feeling it from her heart, and in that small picture, many secrets, depths, are hidden, every picture have story, she had presented in this book.

Index

Chapter-1
A Dream 1

Chapter -2
Face Painting 6

Chapter-3
Berang 10

Chapter-4
On The Water Terrace 13

Chapter-5
Changing Colours 15

Chapter-6
Musik 17

Chapter-7
Painfull Hair 19

Chapter-8
Dhua 21

Chapter-9
I' M The Tree 23

Chapter-10
Wet Cloud 27

Chapter-11
Sunset Point 29

Chapter-12
Walking In Sleeping Position 30

Chapter-13
Life, Fire Ghost & Fun 33

Chapter-14
A Little Bird 35

Chapter - 1
A Dream

I am going somewhere far away in the forest, I am tired of going alone, at a distance there is a ruin Black, black, big stones are like any cave, I was moving towards that cave to avoid the sun rays.

That cave is going as far away from me as I was starting to feel, Eyes were tired, lips were dry from thirst I didn't even know I was helpless, I was going towards that cave to take shelter in the shade.

I could see my shadow too, I was trying to feel the coolness of my shadow by falling to the ground in my own shadow but this is the law of nature, even its own shadow does not support itself.

After touching my shadow, my hands got burnt due to the burning of the hot heat of the ground, so I started getting blister.

I got up and started moving towards the same destination which I was sometimes seen near and far away. Now only thorns were thorns ahead, while passing through a secluded place.

I had to pass through that thorny path and I stopped without stopping, and now as I felt like running away, I ran towards the black stone cave which was still far away.

I still don't know how tall that cave is and whether it's right but I can't seem to find anything.

With no other option for me, the same cave was everything for me at that moment, I tried to speed up my steps and by the end of the evening I reached near the cave of black stone.

That stone was at about 1000m, I was so happy to see him as if I got the treasure. I stayed there for two minutes ... bowed my head to the right-hand side Stared at it for two minutes, there was no one around, only me, and the strong wind which was now giving a little chill as it was evening

Been looking at that black stone cave, now there is no thirst for water Now only the coolness from the winds got peace... It was not so easy to go inside that black stone which seemed to me to be a cave from afar.

That cave which was not like every cave, it was a mountain, made of black strong stones, one could go inside only by lying down between those stones, stones are sharp from above that pricked while crawling and

Today I started moving in the same direction, I kept on falling on the same ground due to stone hit on my head. I felt from inside that by doing anything, I should go to the other side by crawling through the narrow path between the two stones.

Lifting one leg up and grasping it with both hands, I crawled forward crawling my torso through the path between the two shrunken stones.

While crawling, the snake worms had already made their place between the sharp stones from both the sides ... I thought these people could harm me.

I started thinking of myself as the owner of that yard, and the ruler, why don't I consider myself, that I had worked so hard to reach here?

It was dark now; I was tired and I slept between the same two stones. In the morning, the warm wind woke me up.

Now hunger and thirst have compelled me to get out of that place of my rule. And I set out, now I went on the same path as I fought for one night's rule inside the cave between two stones.

I lived in the middle of my reign of a night that passed in the stones with those crawling animals after saying good bye I got out and started on my next unknown path.

And again, the scorching sun, the shadow running ahead of me, seeing that I started laughing... and I sat down in one place.

Looking at my shadow and after a long time I started laughing like a tingle in my brain and I started laughing out loud.

Now I came to know that my shadow has been useful to me in some way and now whenever I got a chance I would talk to my shadow and find it here and there.

Once upon a time, it came to such a point that he had to stand on the back side in the opposite direction and I talk to my own shadow. Today me and my shadow played a game of sun shade it was a lot of fun

And now after this game is done, I move on continued for some time and appeared like a fort from afar. Now I started moving towards that fort and now the thorns also prick my feet which were no longer giving pain.

I reached that fort and it was a big pond, and it was evening now I was looking for my shadow.

Got a little restless that where my shadow was, I understood again, now it is evening, now I will meet my shadow tomorrow morning only by drinking water, I satisfied my water craving, became happy and

Now I started collecting some food items and things to rule my fort, so that no animal should attack me and dominate me.

And about the stone cave of that night, I started thinking about the reign of one day.

Everywhere is deserted, nothing is there, but I understood that I am not alone, my fear has also come such a long way with me on such a difficult path.

I was remembering my shadow that he was with me in the scorching sun was also behind me, but my shadow couldn't cool me down.

But one more thing like when I was happy the fear went somewhere and when I was sad then happiness was far away.

Now I was happy, I was smiling and I woke up I was in my bed, it was morning. My painting is finished at night only.

Thank you for Reading

Chapter - 2
Face Painting

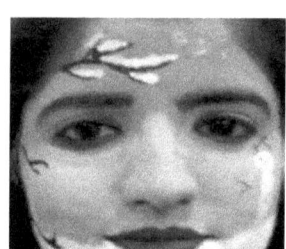

*T*oday I have face painting competition in my office. Group was decided in the office and it would be two people in the group having face of one and one would be painter.

I got a chance to do face painting and I took only two colours' blue and white.

In my childhood, I did clay fruits and colouring on those fruits for art and craft subject in school itself.

After that I am going to do today and did pencil sketches drawing, today I have to do both drawing and painting. That too theme means some message should be.

Now after lunch, bought a colour from a shop that too of only two colours and a brush. Now the time has come where I had to start my painting.

Everyone selected animal theme, some made cat, some made tiger I started making a snowman in the snow on the model's face.

I started painting with the feeling as if I had reached a snowy mountain, my first step in the snowy mountains.

As soon as I stepped on it felt as if the water bales started spreading and I started feeling in the coolness of the water.

As soon as I stepped on it felt as if the lump of water started spreading and I started feeling the coolness of the water. As soon as I put the other foot, I started getting into those lumps of water.

Now the whole body has cooled down, and I was here in the hall, I had a brush in my hand, I had a mixing plate, I started putting blue and white colour in that plate. Now as soon as I started mixing, I felt Snowman is watching me from afar Suddenly that snowman started melting

I panicked and white colour started falling here in the hall, my mentality at that time was to save this white colour, stop it from falling Also, to save that snowman from melting,

I started seeing the thick clouds. That cloud appeared somewhere far away and. Now as soon as I saved this colour from falling, in the same way, this cloud will save that snowman too.

I made the same snowman on the face of the model that I saw in the snowy mountains, The farther I could see the snowman snowflakes, the farther away I made the snowman on the model's face, Now the distance was in my hands.

The distance of both the places was in my hands. I was feeling happy in my heart.

I started making snowman's eyes on the model's face and now both eyes are ready. I had taken the black colour from the office's colleague.

I made black eyes on the face of the model, but at the same time I reached the snowy mountain, then the snowman's eyes were white, there was moisture in the eyes, it was cool I saw that snowman on the snowy hills and now I had to draw the snowman's hands on the model's face, here in the hall.

Now took my brush towards the mixing plate and Now I began to draw the shape of the snowman's hands on the model's face, picking up the white paint with a brush,

Then from the snowy mountain, the snowman began to look at me with his arms outstretched. The brush was in my hands and I put the snowman's hands, that is, put one hand on the other,

I started to feel that what I was doing on the model's face, the snowman is doing the same snowman. Now I put my Santa cap on the snowman head in the mountains and

Now this art was completed, the face painting also seemed complete.

Now the announcement started in the hall and the model and my name were taken, we got the second number.

In the thunder of applause, I reached the same snowy mountains where the snowman was clapping and

After some time that snowman started melting, And I saw that the model was cleaning her face, model washing her face.

Thank you for Reading

Chapter - 3
Berang

I was in search of water but everywhere it was dry, there was no water anywhere, there was no water at any point, after traveling a long distance, I met someone, who himself was very hungry, thirsty and dry, in his hand there was only one wood stick to support him.

He was also suffering from thirst of water, but I was happy to see him, someone showed me in such a deserted place.

And I asked him, did you see any water here? He said there is no water anywhere here, but there are many wells ahead.

My Painting Speaks

I took out the colour box from my bag, took out the pencil and took out the paper to make a picture of the well and went ahead, I was so happy.

He said that I had seen many wells and searched for water but I could not find water. When he got closer, he said there were wells but no water.

Later on, I saw a well, I ran towards it and started moving towards it. I took out the paper from bag, I start painting about the condition of those wells when I was hungry and thirsty.

After that I tried again to go ahead, there were so many wells in one line, there were so many dry wells, Now I made wells with pencil and became happy, now I had to colour, so I went out in search of water.

There were many small wells but there was no water anywhere. Now I myself was thirsty, hungry and now I was tired and I fell there.

Water looked tall, some time it is in very small size, like I was daydreaming, now all night I lay there in a dry place, now the coolness of the night has rewarded me for living a day, as if I lived a day without water, The moonlight of the night cooled me, so that I got up straight in the morning.

As soon as I opened my eyes, small wells were in front of me, I was standing in front of the well, the same small wells and I ran to measure the depth of the well.

I started measuring the depth of many such wells one after the other. There was only depth, there was no water,

There were many wells and they had many deep depths, by measuring them, they came to know about the time. time of measuring their depth.

During the life of those people, the depth of these wells revealed, now I had colours but no water to fill the colours,

Now my painting is complete, I was thinking about the water, to feel the coolness of the water in the painting, and now. My hands spontaneously started to rise upwards towards the sky.

Picking up my bag I went back in the opposite direction, drawing a picture of a girl, she has gone to a well to fill water and she is wearing a very beautiful dress, she has long hair.

The face was filled with colour, the dress was filled with colour and it was the turn of water to make the colour, a glass of water was kept on the table, there were papers, pencils and colours.

It was the turn of the eyes, the water drops falling from the eyes, had to be painted. But no water.

Painting of dry well was done but while colouring, while mixing colours, that glass of water fell from my hands.

water was flowing I tried to stop the water with my hands and my painting well remained dry, only a drop of sweat left, A drop of water.

Thank You for Reading

Chapter - 4
On The Water Terrace

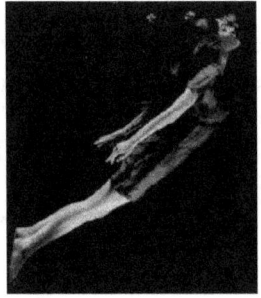

I went for a swim and suddenly a thought popped into my mind, that I should go to the bottom and sit down. And I was now under the water. The blue-blue sky was above that was clearly visible from the clear water I started looking at the sky.

I was wearing white dress, the reflection of white clothes was visible on the water, like white clouds meeting, dividing and dividing itself.

There was a terrace of water over me, and the waves water were coming from the terrace of the water.

I was visible with those waves, in every wave as if the water is telling me something.

As if water is telling me something like I have hidden many faces in this one face. With every wave my image changes, grows and shrinks.

I had a story or my inner soul showed me that this is my identity, this is the law of life, and you are you.

My idol hovering foggy, a white cloud inside the water, my idol was in the water ceiling above me, my image was like white clouds.

My shadow is coming everywhere like a shadow, this shadow was in the roof of the water above, wonderful it was me, my painting a talking picture.

Wonderful it was me, my painting is a talking picture, nature has shown me my reflection in the ceiling of water under water today.

I swam out and I completed my picture with my signature with a brush in my hand, but I could not understand even today that coolness, the terrace of water and the roof of water my shadow.

*** Thank You for Reading ***

Chapter - 5
Changing Colours

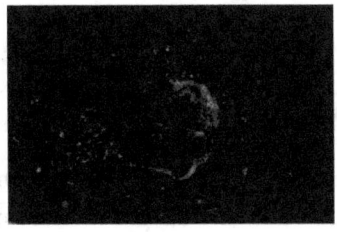

*L*EAF, I have taken green colour today to paint green -green peepal leaves.

Today there was depth of green in that peepal leaf. Today it was the depth of green, in that peepal leaf, there was a smell of green colour.

I kept a green peepal leaf in my book so that I can make a picture of every moment, with the changing day, it fills my eyes with a new feeling. I can bring every layer in the picture.

Started seeing that leaf kept in the book every day.

After the day was gone, today that green colour was no longer dark and I had to change my colour to green, didn't even have the smell that could be felt in my painting.

After two or three days I opened my book and saw today peepal leaf has turned yellow. I have felt the changing colours in my painting.

Now day by day the colour of the leaves is starting to fade Now day by day the colour of the leaf is starting to fade, now the peepal leaf has dried up, it has become hard.

The falling portions in the book of Peepal leaves remained the same, completely dried up

Now the water started appearing in the peepal leaf, there were lattice in leaves, there were tiny holes in the reticulated leaf.

Many lines were flowing, there was a stream of life in it, now it has been painted with golden colour, now it is a gold leaf but there is no life.

Even today and every day I have to change colours to add colour to my painting, this peepal leaf tells the depths of life. Colours exist but life ends here.

Thank You for Reading

Chapter - 6
Musik

I was going by four-wheeler, through the mountains covered in many green grass rugs far and wide.

Waterfalls were flowing from the mountains like swirls, after stopping the car, I went to a river bank and stopped and I sat down.

The sound of the wind is like sssas sas sa si si si... The sound of the branches colliding with the trees nearby.

The sound of the rapid flow of water, the sudden landing of the neighbours on the ground and the sound of tumbling.

Nature said sing like me my steps started the sound of dry leaves falling under my feet, a new tune was given, a part of painting was given I suddenly got scared by the sound of some birds moving forward. I got a new tune.

Fluttering sound of birds, the sound of feet stopping, the sound of walking, the wind is also there.

Then someone said tiger is coming from front, When I turned, the tiger was in front of me, his eyes were staring at me.

Now the tiger started moving towards me, my heartbeat started getting faster. The heart was beating fast and the tune was very loud, the tiger was not ready to take its eyes off.

Then the sun was about to set, the cold wind started coming, the beating stopped, there was peace in the mind, but there was also a tiger in front.

I was with my paint brush and the tiger was moving away in my painting, my tune is done

Thank You for Reading

Chapter - 7
Painfull Hair

 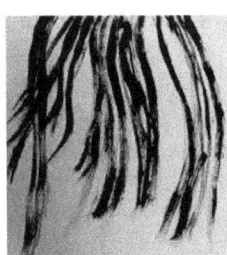

Today I reached the office early and my office-mate has also arrived. I put the bag on my table and went back to the chair and went to the office-mate in the other cabin.

Now when I came back my office-mate sat on my chair and she got up and started leaving and then I grabbed the head pad of the chair with my hands to pull the chair.

The office-mate's hair was lying on the head pad of that chair, some part of his long thick black hair was there, Who I don't see in a hurry.

And I pulled the chair towards me, her hair was already on the chair, her hair got pressed because of holding hands,

The sound of screaming came from his mouth, I thought something had happened, but he said it was because of you and you injured my hair.

This was new to me, hair doesn't feel at all and long hair was on my forehead, there might be a slight stretch.

There is no wound, I feel like drawing blood, I became very sad, I said sorry and started making my painting

There was no blood coming out of the hair, but I could feel its pain, and I came to know from the people that the office mate's hair has feelings like body skin.

That day his painful hair, the wound on his hair, because of me. The unheard story of a pain that can only be felt.

She cuts means trim her long black thick hair once in 15 days with someone's help, a painful tale of normal looking hair.

For Me It Was a Miraculous Event and Stop Me Here, Invisible Wound in My Painting.

Thank You for Reading

Chapter - 8
Dhua

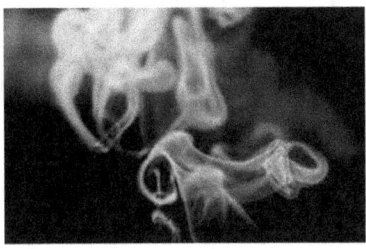

I was worshiping at home, I offered flowers, now lit a lamp, and also lit incense sticks. After a while that smoke started moving towards me.

Suddenly it started changing its shape, white clouds were following me.

Coming to the smoke, she was now look like a girl with a tail whose tail was attached to incense sticks. I decided to let this smoke descend into my painting.

That smoke changed many shapes. So much power in the wood of an incense stick, it was the result of the combination of both the smoke of the incense stick and the surrounding air.

It is the result of the synergy of both, as if they were made for each other, they are making this shape with the help of each other.

With perfect balance, with each other's support, the result of the work done is this beautiful shape.

The smoke of incense sticks knew me as if they wanted to say something to me and the winds too, I felt that my own picture was prepared in the aura, and was made, and has been shown to me, their love for me so much, thank you so much.

From my photography, my painting was completed, but I could not find such a beautiful perfect balance anywhere.

I got a chance to use white colour here too, this colour is made up of the inter-soul of so many colours and the combination of many colours. Many forms of the same colour, and rhythm with the wind.

Thank You for Reading

Chapter - 9
I' M The Tree

A very beautiful museum, I Came and stopped at an iconic statue and then.

I used to live in town as a child, near our railway quarters there was a very big very old or old banyan tree. I went to that banyan tree many times, the first time I got scared.

Now after going a couple of times, my fear is gone, now I think this tree was very big according to me, but I felt that I should make friends.

I made a picture remembering its behaviour in childhood and that picture was still incomplete,

A few days later, on a summer vacation, someone hung a swing made of a bicycle tire so that everyone could take a tall swing.

Now I would also hang from that swing, sometimes I would swing a long swing, sometimes I would turn upside down.

I had long thick hair and since my hair was wet after washing, I would have got a chance to keep my hair loose.

And with the same wet hair, I started moving towards that swing, happy while shaking the hair, I reached near the banyan tree.

It was a swing, I hung upside down and after some time sat down with the roots of the banyan tree, its root was hard but in wavy shaped, like curly hair like open hair

It was a swing, I hung upside down and after some time sat down with the roots of the banyan tree, the roots were rough.

Now looking up at banyan tree, its own roots upside down, seems hanging roots, I held those roots and played for a long time, and now I turned upside down in the swing Now the roots of the banyan tree and my hair were the same.

I thought that this banyan tree was me, now every time I used to go near the banyan tree in this, I used to find myself like that banyan tree.

Under the banyan tree, the leaves swayed with the wind, I too used to swing with the wind.

In the rain, the banyan tree used to get drenched and then dried up, I too used to get wet with rain water during the rainy days and then I also used to dry up.

Nothing different. Emotions were also the same. Few things were different, but I used to find myself in him, I was that tree.

I feel My hands are like tree branches.

I am now convinced that this is not a banyan tree, it is me. If you turn the banyan tree upside down, then that banyan tree is like me, and if you turn me upside down then I am like that banyan tree,

My hair is like a banyan tree, or the roots of a banyan tree are like my hair. After many years I made a painting of the same banyan tree.

When I saw the Statue of a wooden woman kept in a museum, hidden picture of a girl in some part of the tree, I thought it was my picture.

Trying to put the same feeling in my painting today. Now I am happy in painting like the weather and in front of the banyan tree like a banyan tree.

Now I have lived every season, in my painting, considering myself as a banyan tree, wrapped in a tree, feeling the same.

My hair had sensations like the roots of a banyan tree, my hair, my skin, could absorb water, just like a banyan tree could absorb water, I start swinging by being engrossed in myself, just like a banyan tree swings.

Sometimes I have got drenched in the rain, sometimes I have blossomed, sometimes I am feeling cool in winter and sometimes I have become dry. Due to dryness, today someone has come to cut me.

Some people have also come to save me from being cut. But no one took pity on me, nor did those people stop.

Those people were cutting the tree, I was in pain, the tears of the tree, now they have become my tears.

I completed my painting and now whenever I see trees cut, whenever I see a tree being cut I feel that some part of my body is being cut.

Now I was dead and I was in a museum as a statue of beautiful woman, "My Painting Speaks" I'm done.

Thank You for Reading

Chapter - 10
Wet Cloud

I went for a walk in the hills with my hostel friends, it was better than what I had heard. In the morning we went, the car going through the mountains, cold wind and sudden rain.

They were roasting the corn, hot corn, hot -hot tea and rain, were eating corn soaked, after taking a sip of tea, now the weather has become more beautiful.

Now there was the sound of thunder of clouds, from that voice came from near the ear, as if there is a speaker near the ear, we were at such a height that now it was starting to breathe a little.

Now after the sound stopped, we started roaming in the mountains and very beautiful hills and changes were also getting closer.

standing in front, we could neither see nor hear each other, we were in the midst of such thick clouds.

After the clouds went away slowly, I started painting now standing in the midst of high mountains, I was caught between the clouds coming and going, and those wet clouds soaked me and on the side were green grass, yellow-coloured flowers like a rug of flowers. I took photography here.

*** Thank You for Reading ***

Chapter - 11
Sunset Point

I reached Sunset Point, and I felt Sunset Point from afar, as if I was entering a painting inside a painting. Nature has already made a painting and I am entering that painting.

Sky candle hanging in the air. An orange-coloured sphere and a dark cloud surrounding it is visible from afar and I am looking at the sun from a fort.

Thank You for Reading

Chapter - 12
Walking In Sleeping Position

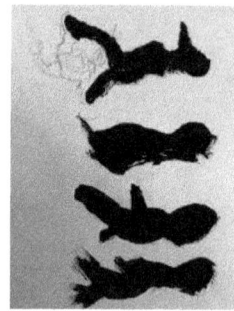

Many animals were walking together, walking in a line, not standing, but in sleeping position, like sleeping on the bed, I did not see people lying down and walking,

We were walking in speed. If someone walks like a normal human standing upright, then that will die, so they have to walk in sleeping position.

We were all like a wooden branch, neither eyes nor ears, just a twig... nor any sensation Just walking, roaming, walking with our leader, our shape kept changing with every step. Sometimes we looked like a bridge.

They just have to live and they don't know what to do to live. Leader was just walking in sleeping position, now someone tasted the food and saw the taste of food was very bad, the leader felt bad, so no one touched that food. And went ahead.

Now everyone started following the leader, don't know who they are called, but the leader knows and he was in search of water.

At one place there was a small pond of water, that water was like red coloured blood. The leader drank and saw that the taste was bad

Meanwhile, sometimes we used to play a game of blind eye with our leader, we rarely saw our leader, and he did not say anything.

They all went ahead, started chasing the leader, the leader felt hungry and thirsty, and everyone only followed him.

Ongoing forward with the leader got water, the leader drank the water, now seeing the leader everyone drank the water and everyone started moving forward.

And now we all came out crossing the river from inside the river, the leader was half submerged and we were on the waves of water.

Ongoing forward, an animal appeared, the leader ate it, all stood silently Now after going a little far, everyone was hungry, everyone was watching and the leader was getting smaller.

Now all here and there, were divided into small pieces. Slowly Somebody is eating the leader and we were all fainting

In the morning again the leader came and stood, and again everyone started walking happily, walking in the sleeping position together.

But now all the leaders were walking in standing position. we were still walking in sleeping position.

Thank You for Reading

Chapter - 13
Life, Fire Ghost & Fun

 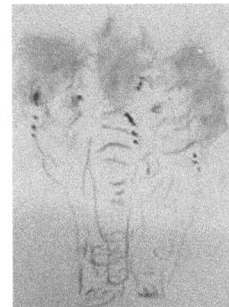

An elephant has gone on a walk in the forest after being engrossed, and suddenly a ball of fire started to appear, it had come to give pain, had come to burn.

The elephant was saving itself. The brush of my painting was also moving just like the elephant is saving itself, the elephant in my painting.

Now that elephant has become a fat size in my painting. Now I am reducing the size of the elephant.

Now I reduced the size and I didn't have paint colours, other colours were red, yellow colour only

From that I started painting on the elephant's ear to make the ears smaller. Picked up and painted red colour with a brush, gave colour to the elephant's ear. Now given yellow colour, now the size of the elephant seemed small.

That tv news was in my mind and now it is in my painting.

What was the need to add red yellow colour to the elephant, I could have stayed one day but, why today? Was this someone's conspiracy?

It was not a red colour, it was a ball of fire, it was a fire ghost, it changes shape, sometimes it goes back sometimes forward, it starts moving back and forth with the winds and

The elephant that is capricious, is a happy animal, has become a victim of someone's conspiracy.

There were tears in someone's eyes, there was happiness in someone's eyes, somewhere there was silence, somewhere there was a celebration.

I never had this colour in my colours, today only the burning animal had to be painted. There was a moment of happiness, and now there is only silence of sorrows, the end of a living being.

Thank You for Reading

Chapter - 14
A Little Bird

It was the rainy season, all the mountains were wet, the streams of water were falling down the hill. Some children hid in a cave inside the mountains to escape the rain.

Now rain on all sides and clouds, dark clouds and winds made their stand on the hill, camped, now they started fighting each other as they started colliding.

Now it was not a drop of rain, it was a stream of water, The water slowly started going into the caves and now it is night in the morning, a bird saw some children inside.

She started digging the mountain from above. She wanted to save those children; she was small but had big heart, strong thoughts in her, A little bird.

Thank You For Reading

Epilogue

*E*very colour and world of nature tells some story, there's a story hidden behind every picture. There is a story from heart to pain that gives relief to the eyes.

I ruled inside the cave for a day on snakes, some insects, lizards, my hunger forced me to leave the kingdom.

There was painting in the morning and I was also at home. A red coloured ghost climbed on him, he cried, shouted, here he started running but …that red ghost wins.

With each of his blows, the body slowly broke into pieces, Beauty appeared to him, in the glass panes.

Seeing him sinking, pressing down, seeing him, the little bird got up, ran, ran and started examining the mountains and digging the mountain to save them.

Author's Note

The miraculous things we see but don't feel, every painting makes you feel pain, happiness. A momentary pain, this is my experience I want to share my experience through this book "My Painting Speaks"

I collected ideas from many different places during my journey, I got few outstanding thoughts I want to put my experience in sketch.

Thank You for The Inspiration!

Author's Note

I have immersed some moments of my life in my art painting, I have done painting since childhood, such as pencil sketch, painting, face painting etc.

The experience I used to feel while hand sketches, paper painting, and face painting, that experience, that inner voice tells something that is written in this book. Every painting of mine tells a new story,

Every painting of mine, every painting takes me to some depth, and carries a deep message.

I wanted to share my story with the world and so I have written this book "My Painting Speaks" and I hope you will adore it.

Thank you again for your support!

www.ingramcontent.com/pod-product-compliance
Lightning Source LLC
La Vergne TN
LVHW010620070526
838199LV00063BA/5215